Super Sentences & Perfect Paragraphs

by Mack Lewis

New York • Toronto • London • Auckland • Sydney
Mexico City • New Delhi • Hong Kong • Buenos Aires

Teaching *Resources*

To Darryl and Dain
I am who I am because of who you've been

Scholastic Inc. grants teachers permission to photocopy the reproducible pages from this book for classroom use. No other part of this publication may be reproduced in whole or in part, or stored in a retrieval system, or transmitted in any form or by any means, electronic, mechanical, photocopying, recording, or otherwise, without written permission of the publisher. For information regarding permission, write to Scholastic Inc., 557 Broadway, New York, NY 10012.

Editor: Maria L. Chang
Cover and interior design: Holly Grundon
Illustrations: Mike Moran

ISBN-13: 978-0-545-06403-3
ISBN-10: 0-545-06403-1
Copyright © 2009 by Mack Lewis
Printed in the U.S.A.

4 5 6 7 8 9 10   40   15 14 13 12

Contents

Super Sentences Reproducible Pages

Perfect Paragraphs Reproducible Pages

Basic Paragraph Paste-Ups

Basic Paragraph Rewrites

Intermediate Paragraph Paste-Ups

Intermediate Paragraph Rewrites

Advanced Paragraph Rewrites

Multi-Paragraph Projects

Perfect Paragraph Templates

Introduction

Writing is one of the most difficult subjects to teach and therefore one of the most neglected areas of instruction. Teachers fall into the habit of merely assigning topics and fretting over the poor results. Students are prone to resisting instruction and whining, "I can't think of anything to write!" In this era of high-stakes testing, it has become more important than ever that teachers have an effective and easy-to-use writing program.

These straightforward, reproducible daily and weekly lessons will help turn students into thoughtful, accurate writers and prepare them for standardized writing tests. Because I've used these activities with my own students, I know kids enjoy them. When it's time to write, there'll be no moaning and groaning—from the students or the teachers! In fact, those who have used my approach say the Super Sentence activity is the best 15 minutes of their day.

Because the sentence is the foundation of quality writing, I've developed a simple format with which teachers can instruct students on writing exquisite individual sentences. Consider how frequently the sentence "It was fun" mars a child's essay, or how often a weak command of punctuation results in a "peppering" of stray marks. This typically points to a lack of emphasis or a boring, textbook approach to grammar. My Super Sentence approach makes it easy for teachers to deliver fun, engaging daily lessons on writing great sentences on any subject. Furthermore, this approach gets at different kinds of sentences, including compound, dialogue, fact-based, metaphorical, and many more. To further support each lesson, I've also included a weekly Word Wall Idea.

The Perfect Paragraph format is familiar to readers of Scholastic's *Storyworks* magazine, where it is a regular feature. I've put together a different lesson for each week of the school year. Each one provides a writing prompt and gives students practice working with standard structures in each of six modes. After using them, your students should be able to quickly and easily draft multi-paragraph essays on nearly any subject.

I recall reading in a teacher's guide from *Storyworks* a recommendation that said something like "If you want your students to be strong writers, have them write every day." Every day? Of course, we all know that writing is one of the most difficult and time-consuming subjects to teach. It requires lots of one-on-one conferencing, a ton of patience, and, most of all, more time than any of us has to assess it. Every day may seem impossible, but with *Super Sentences and Perfect Paragraphs*, purposeful, enjoyable, and effective writing lessons are an everyday reality.

How to Use Super Sentences

1. **Introduce Sentence Structure of the Week.** On *Monday* (or the first day of the week), introduce the new sentence structure (such as Sentence Containing Dialogue) by posting the sample sentence and reviewing the hints from the reproducible worksheet. Make photocopies of the worksheet and distribute the top half to each student.

2. **Select Topics.** Invite students to select two or three topics to write about. You can have them choose from the list on page 9, assign the topics, or generate a few ideas with the class. Topics should range from silly ("Orangutans with bad haircuts") to serious ("Climate change"), and from simple ("Shower caps") to complex ("What it means to be a true friend"). While it's important to allow students some freedom to select "off the wall" topics as this increases their engagement, it's also critical to periodically introduce serious topics.

3. **Craft Sentences.** Give students time to craft their own sentences, then ask for volunteers to post their finished product for discussion.

4. **Post and Discuss.** Post two or three student-created sentences and invite the class to comment on, compliment, and criticize the sentences. Guide the class to help them pose criticism politely and constructively. While editing for conventions is a part of this process, be sure to lead the class toward discussing the structure of the sentence, the use of details, word choice, and application of the "hints" from the worksheet. If time allows, you can also quickly read aloud more student sentences, but save a few to introduce the next day's lesson.

5. **Repeat.** From *Tuesday through Thursday*, repeat the lesson, focusing on the same sentence structure but with new topics. Instead of posting the sentence sample from the worksheet, select a sentence from the previous day's student work. Try to pick one (from an anonymous student) that demonstrates a common writing problem or that highlights a favorable trait. Using another copy of the same worksheet (or a sheet of notebook paper), have students each write a new Super Sentence with the same structure. Post one or two on the board for discussion.

6. **Test and Assess.** On *Friday*, distribute copies of the bottom half of the reproducible worksheet and have students use this "test" worksheet to draft a Super Sentence for formal evaluation. Insist that sentences be error free as defined by grade-level standards. For example, the spelling of age-appropriate words should be correct (or, at your discretion, if dictionaries are available, students can use them to ensure correct spelling of all words) and grade-appropriate punctuation should be accurate. By using the Super Sentence method, students can and will produce correct, detailed, enjoyable sentences consistently.

How to Get the Most Out of Super Sentences

Pacing

Moving rapidly through the activity is important. While a lesson may take a little longer early in the school year, it should take only about 20 to 25 minutes on Monday and 15 minutes the rest of the week. Friday's test could be as little as five minutes depending upon the level of the class and whether or not you choose to post and discuss student-generated sentences from the test.

Free the Inner Writer

Model for your students that these sentences need not be realistic. Whether fiction or nonfiction, serious or silly, the emphasis is on sentence construction and spontaneity. Periodically post your own sentences that are as entertaining as they are correct. Be sure to write about your students and yourself in fun ways while commending your students for being good sports. However, because young people tend to have difficulty understanding the limits of good-natured ribbing, set clear standards about allowing students to write about their classmates.

Respect Feelings

Students love to put words in the mouths of their classmates during the dialogue lessons. My students and I call these "quote wars." Here, especially, you will need to set standards for appropriateness and hold discussions about the difference between good-natured ribbing and focusing on another person's "flaws." When the class is having difficulty respecting boundaries, try teaching them to use the formatting device of putting a single capital letter followed by a blank line: "My supplier for Barbie doll accessories went out of business," moaned M_____.

Have Fun With Topics

Teach your students to make any given topic work for them. For example, if the topic is "elves" but the student wants to write about video games, encourage him or her to write a sentence about an elf who is playing a video game. In so doing, you'll teach students to fearlessly tackle any topic. Few will say, "I can't think of anything to write" or "I don't like any of the topics."

Use Word Walls

Each weekly Super Sentence reproducible includes a suggestion for a word wall supporting the given sentence concept. Some word walls are meant to stay posted for a week or two, while others may be left up for the entire year. Simply take a sheet of butcher paper and post it where students can reach. Experiment with different ways to introduce the given concept, then invite students to add words as they discover them. Be sure to regularly revisit each wall to discuss what students have been posting. If you have dry-erase markers and a large window in the classroom, using the glass as a word wall increases student interest. Finally, walls such as the Word Cemetery and Danger Words are of more permanent importance, so a little artistic flare is helpful.

A Sampling of Super Sentence Topics

Whether assigned by you or volunteered by students, Super Sentence topics should cover a wide array of ideas and should vary in seriousness. It's amazing what kids can do with the topics listed below! Try writing them on cards and putting them in a container so students can draw cards as needed.

Animals that eat humans
When the teacher overslept
Global warming
Worms
Pizza
Chicken pox
Chores
Cheerleaders
SpongeBob SquarePants
Horses
Buying new clothes
Allowance
If pigs could fly
The tooth fairy
Shower caps
Runny noses
Barbie dolls
Chicken nuggets
Being grounded
Straitjackets
Kissing
Christmas
Handball
Sharing a bedroom
Skipping rope on a pogo stick
Cell phones
Disneyland
The rain forest
The Mississippi River
Tidal waves
Hurricanes
Bad-hair days
Giraffes that eat quiche
AstroTurf
Fire drills
Bats
Asteroids

Dating
Love notes
Favorite animals
Street hockey
Fast cars
Kindness
Guts
When buzzards attack
GI Joe
The Pittsburgh Steelers
   (or your local team)
Oprah
Bullies
Winning the lottery
Video games
Superman's tights
Favorite authors
Chicago (or any other city)
Bugs that attack kids
Wheatgrass
Bad food you had to eat
Staying home with a fever
Toilet training
Cats
Alarm clocks
Prison
Mr. President
Cornbread
War
Mashed potatoes
Air bags
Old Maid
Tutus
Soccer in a blizzard
Ticks
Deodorant
Yellowstone

Mistakes in the kitchen
Mean girls
Aliens
Ex-planet Pluto
When the dog drank from the toilet
Mexico
Fast-talking teens
Rainy days
Legos
Purses
Christopher Columbus
Aircraft carriers
Dirt
Microscopes
Guitars
Rats that can read
Little House on the Prairie
Sleepovers
Moms
Being stuck on a lifeboat
Breakfast cereal
Friendship
Sticks and stones
Hannah Montana
Warts
Warthogs
Quarterbacks
Maple leaves
Cribs
Monsters in the closet
Bacon and eggs
Celery sticks
My Uncle Alfredo
All-star games
Moving away
Harry Potter
"Make my day"

How to Use Perfect Paragraphs

Before Pablo Picasso developed his own unique style, he honed his craft by imitating the work of others. The Perfect Paragraph activities in this book are based on this same imitative principle. By using the templates, color-coding, topics, and examples in this section, you'll be helping your students improve their writing so that the Picasso in each of them can eventually break free.

Ready-to-Use Templates

When students are writing rough drafts, have them use the Perfect Paragraph templates (pages 89–92). The benefits of having kids write individual sentences in individual boxes on a template will quickly become apparent. With the help of these templates, students will be more adept at differentiating between events and details, recognizing boring sentences such as "It was fun," and spotting mechanical errors. Editing one box at a time also encourages them to be more thorough. Once students become comfortable using templates, have them begin to create their own using 12" x 18" white construction paper, which can be folded and used to store their drafts. Creating their own writing template is a particularly important skill to develop before tackling standardized writing tests. Offering students a preprinted template is generally prohibited, but giving them time to make and use their own is usually within the rules.

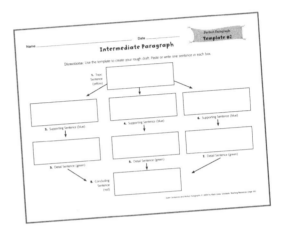

Color Coding Sentences

Have students color code both the sequencing activities and their rough drafts. Not only will this help them distinguish between topic sentences (*yellow*), supporting sentences (*blue*), detail sentences (*green*), and concluding sentences (*red*), it will also train them to look closely at individual sentences for meaning, conventions, and word choice. The color-coding pattern used here matches that of Scholastic's *Storyworks* magazine. However, feel free to adjust the colors to match any program you or your school might have already adopted simply by "whiting out" the colors listed on each reproducible and writing in those that meet your needs. Consistency is key. As students use this program, the label "blue sentence" will take on a specific meaning. Don't confuse them by changing colors from one program to the next.

Direct Instruction and Discussion

This program was not designed to be merely a seatwork filler activity. While the sequencing pages may be completed as seatwork, direct instruction and discussion are equally important. You can prewrite the sentences on sheets of 3" x 18" tagboard and have the class (or small groups) sequence them using a pocket chart or bulletin board. Post a small colored card to the left of each sentence for color coding. You can also create transparencies of the reproducible and complete them on the overhead. Use either approach in lieu of the reproducible sheet or as a post-activity review. Discuss what characterizes a detail sentence as opposed to a supporting sentence. What word clues help identify the sequence? Talk freely about what students like and dislike about the sample paragraphs. Are there boring words? Are there phrases that could be improved upon? Are there clichés? In the Intermediate Paragraph Paste-Up activities (pages 65–70), an extra, unnecessary sentence is included. Encourage students to discuss why it doesn't belong.

Vocabulary that Works for You

Note that supporting sentences can go by different names. You might call them "reason-why" sentences when they're explaining why the topic sentence is true, such as in a persuasive or descriptive piece. Or you might call them "event" sentences when they're part of a sequence of events, such as in the narrative or imaginative mode. As you continue to teach the writing process, no doubt you'll land on additional terminology that works for you and your students, but always identify each as a type of "supporting sentence" that require consistent color coding.

Multi-Paragraph Essays

The final section includes six writing tasks for a multi-paragraph paper to be drafted using an enlarged copy of Template #4 (page 92) or student-created templates/writing folders. Consider collecting the finished stories from each task into a themed classroom anthology. You can also build on earlier Perfect Paragraph activities. Expand single paragraphs into multi-paragraph papers by using each original supporting sentence as the topic sentence of a new paragraph.

I hope you and your students enjoy this book and find it useful. To find more teaching tips, offer feedback, or post your students' best Super Sentences and Perfect Paragraphs, please visit my Web site at http://www.SuperSentences.com.

A Daily Approach to Writing

Day	Super Sentencing *(15 to 20 minutes per day)*	Perfect Paragraphing *(15 to 20 minutes per day)*
Mon.	• Introduce the sentence structure using the reproducible. • Have each student write one sentence. • Post two or three sentences for discussion, emphasizing how we can learn from our mistakes.	• Assign paragraph sequencing activity, such as a "Basic Paragraph Rewrite" reproducible. • Have students complete worksheet as seatwork.
Tue.	• Select student samples from the previous day, focusing on common errors and favorable traits, and post them for discussion. • Have students draft new samples on notebook paper. • Post two or three new sentences for discussion.	• Write sentences from the previous day's lesson on 3" x 18" tagboard sheets. • Use direct instruction to review the paragraph, encouraging the class to correctly re-sequence the sentences. • Guide the class to discuss why the correct order makes sense, emphasizing the structural components and word clues.
Wed.	• Repeat the activities from Tuesday, again highlighting common errors and favorable traits from student samples. • Have students draft new samples using new topics. • Post two or three new sentences for discussion.	• Post tagboard from Tuesday's lesson where students can revisit it. • Briefly review the lesson. • Have students write their rough drafts using a reproducible template. Emphasize one sentence per box. • Have students color-code their drafts.
Thur.	• Post and review more student samples. • Have each student draft one new sentence for formal evaluation on the reproducible sheet. • Again post one or two student sentences for evaluation, asking, *"Does this meet the standard for a sentence? Why or why not?"*	• Have students edit and revise their paragraphs one sentence at a time. If using a reproducible template, edit one box at a time. • As time allows, have students begin writing their final drafts on notebook paper or computer.
Fri.	• Have students "repair" their sentence tests on the back of the test or on notebook paper as per class standards. • Invite students to post their corrected sentences on a classroom bulletin board or Web site.	• Have students complete their final drafts. • Invite students to share and post their finished paragraphs on a classroom bulletin board or Web site.

Name _____ Date _____

Standard Sentence

Excellent Example: My friend Larry likes to put pickles on his pepperoni pizza.

Helpful Hints: Remember the rules for a sentence: It must start with a capital letter, end with the appropriate ending punctuation, tell who or what the sentence is about, and tell what happened. It must also be a complete thought that makes sense.

Now write your own standard sentence:

_____

_____

_____

_____

✂

Super Sentence Test

Name _____ · Date _____

Standard Sentence

Write your own standard sentence:

_____

_____

_____

_____

Word Wall Idea: *What's in a sentence? Make a list of all the parts and pieces of a sentence, including not only the basics, such as* periods *and* nouns, *but other less common concepts such as* quotation marks, adverbs, *and* contractions. *Leave the list up all year and add to it as new "construction tools" are discovered.*

Practice

Standard Sentence

Magnificent Model: Whenever my little sister, Cindy, watches *Sesame Street*, she always sucks on her big toe.

Red-Hot Reminders: Standard sentences don't have to be simple or short, but always double-check to make sure you've followed the rules for a sentence. Also, avoid boring words and words that get used too much.

Now write your own standard sentence:

_____

_____

_____

✂

Super Sentence
Test

Name _____   Date _____

Standard Sentence

Write your own standard sentence:

_____

_____

_____

_____

Word Wall Idea: *Make a Word Cemetery — a list of overused or boring words to avoid, such as* fun, cool, *and* stuff. *Add to the Word Cemetery all year long as you encounter more words that are best laid to rest in peace.*

Name _____   Date _____

Detailed Standard Sentence

Exceptional Exemplar: Yesterday my little brother spent his entire allowance on pink and green polka-dotted pajamas at Macy's.

Nifty Notes: Add detail by including some of "The Five W's": *who, what, where, when,* and *why.* How many can you find in the sample sentence? Don't forget to double-check your capitals and end marks!

Now write your own detailed sentence:

_____

_____

_____

Super Sentences and Perfect Paragraphs © 2009 by Mack Lewis. Scholastic Teaching Resources

✂

Super Sentence
Test

Name _____   Date _____

Detailed Standard Sentence

Write your own detailed sentence:

_____

_____

_____

_____

Super Sentences and Perfect Paragraphs © 2009 by Mack Lewis. Scholastic Teaching Resources

Word Wall Idea: *List adjectives that add spice to writing, such as* polka-dotted.

Name _____   Date _____

Detailed Standard Sentence

Sensational Sample: When we go out for a fancy dinner in the city, we always search frantically for a top-notch steak house because my Uncle Charlie loves a juicy T-bone.

Reliable Rule of Thumb: Add detail by being specific (*T-bone* instead of just *steak*, *Uncle Charlie* instead of just *uncle*), and increase interest by using an occasional adjective (such as *juicy*) or adverb (such as *frantically*).

Now write your own detailed sentence:

_____

_____

_____

✂

Super Sentence Test

Name _____   Date _____

Detailed Standard Sentence

Write your own detailed sentence:

_____

_____

_____

_____

Word Wall Idea: *List adverbs that set the mood, such as* frantically.

Name _____   Date _____

Compound Sentence

Satisfying Specimen: The warmer summer weather is disappearing quickly, *but* it's okay because I like how the leaves change color in the fall.

Apt Advice: A *compound sentence* often combines two sentences with a comma and "joining word" such as *and, but, so, yet*, or *because*. If you replace the comma and joining word with a period, you should have two complete sentences.

Now write your own compound sentence:

_____

_____

_____

Super Sentences and Perfect Paragraphs © 2009 by Mack Lewis. Scholastic Teaching Resources

- ✁

Super Sentence Test

Name _____   Date _____

Compound Sentence

Write your own compound sentence:

_____

_____

_____

_____

Super Sentences and Perfect Paragraphs © 2009 by Mack Lewis. Scholastic Teaching Resources

- -

Word Wall Idea: Make a list of joining words—also known as conjunctions—*such as* and, so, *and* but *(a very short list, which is precisely the point).*

Name _____ Date _____

Sentence Using a Semicolon

Must-See Model: When I went hiking in the Appalachian Mountains I found two ticks under my arm; I guess they're pretty common up there.

Inspirational Ideas: When two independent sentences are closely related, you can join them with a semicolon instead of a joining word. To make sure it works, try replacing the semicolon with a joining word such as *and* or *but*. Don't forget your details!

Now write your own sentence using a semicolon:

_____

_____

_____

Super Sentence Test

Name _____ Date _____

Sentence Using a Semicolon

Write your own sentence using a semicolon:

_____

_____

_____

_____

Word Wall Idea: *Make a list of Danger Words — commonly misused or misspelled words such as* then, because, like, *and* plus. *Add to it all year as new dangers are uncovered!*

Name _____ Date _____

Sentence Containing Dialogue

Entertaining Example: "Yesterday I went to the toy store and bought lots of new outfits for my Barbie dolls," said Jimmy.

Hypnotic Hints: By using quotation marks, you can put words in other people's mouths. Surround the spoken words with quotation marks. The first quotation mark shows when a person begins talking, and the second one shows when he or she stops. Try thinking of them as an "open mouth" and a "closed mouth."

What silly thing might someone say? Write your own dialogue sentence:

_____

_____

_____

- ✂

Super Sentence Test

Name _____ Date _____

Sentence Containing Dialogue

Write your own dialogue sentence:

_____

_____

_____

_____

- -

Word Wall Idea: *List contractions, which tend to make dialogue ring true.*

Name _____   Date _____

Dialogue Sentence With Alternate Tag

Insightful Sample: "Hannah Montana is just so dreamy," sighed Zach as he stared at her latest CD.

Rip-Roaring Recommendations: Experiment with *tags* other than the word *said*. Words like *yapped*, *bellowed*, or any of a hundred others add meaning by telling *how* someone spoke. Also, be sure to set off what was said with a comma, and feel free to set the scene by telling when or where.

Now write your own dialogue sentence with an alternate tag:

_____

_____

_____

_____

✂

Super Sentence Test

Name _____   Date _____

Dialogue Sentence With Alternate Tag

Write your own dialogue sentence with an alternate tag:

_____

_____

_____

_____

Word Wall Idea: *List alternatives to the word* said, *such as* muttered, yelled, *and* sighed.

Name _____   Date _____

Dialogue Sentence
With the Speaker at the Beginning

Delightful Demo: When Ambyr saw a giraffe walk past her window, she boomed, "Dad, the horses are having a wild party again!"

Warnings for the Wise: You still need to set off the tag from the "open mouth" with a comma. Notice, too, that what the speaker says is a sentence by itself. It starts with a capital letter and ends with ending punctuation *inside* the quotation marks!

Now write your own dialogue sentence with the speaker at the beginning:

_____

_____

_____

Super Sentences and Perfect Paragraphs © 2009 by Mack Lewis. Scholastic Teaching Resources

- ✂

Super Sentence Test

Name _____   Date _____

Dialogue Sentence
With the Speaker at the Beginning

Write your own dialogue sentence with the speaker at the beginning:

_____

_____

_____

Super Sentences and Perfect Paragraphs © 2009 by Mack Lewis. Scholastic Teaching Resources

- -

Word Wall Idea: *List more alternatives to the word* said, *such as* growled, teased, *and* cried. *There are so many, it's worth continuing!*

Practice

Sentence With an Indirect Quotation

Imaginative Model: After he graded the geometry exam, Mr. Sanchez said that my tessellations were the best he'd seen in years.

Artful Advice: When you put what someone else said into your own words (for example, when summarizing), it is called an *indirect quotation*. In such cases, leave the quotation marks out.

Now write your own indirect quotation:

_____

_____

_____

_____

Super Sentences and Perfect Paragraphs © 2009 by Mack Lewis. Scholastic Teaching Resources

----

Super Sentence Test

Name _____ Date _____

Sentence With an Indirect Quotation

Write your own indirect quotation:

_____

_____

_____

_____

Super Sentences and Perfect Paragraphs © 2009 by Mack Lewis. Scholastic Teaching Resources

Word Wall Idea: *List math vocabulary.*

Name _____ Date _____

Sentence With a Compound Subject

Near-Perfect Prototype: The Brooklyn Street Bell Chorus entertained us at a holiday event in the basement of the church. The guy who owns the comic-book store did too. **Better:** The Brooklyn Street Bell Chorus and the guy who owns the comic-book store entertained us at a holiday event in the basement of the church.

Tantalizing Thought: When there is more than one *subject* (the who or what of the sentence) performing the same action, you can combine them. However, be careful what order you put them in. Would the Near-Perfect Prototype still have the same meaning if the two subjects were reversed?

Now write your own compound-subject sentence:

_____

_____

_____

Super Sentences and Perfect Paragraphs © 2009 by Mack Lewis. Scholastic Teaching Resources

- ✂

Super Sentence Test

Name _____ Date _____

Sentence With a Compound Subject

Write your own compound-subject sentence:

_____

_____

_____

_____

Super Sentences and Perfect Paragraphs © 2009 by Mack Lewis. Scholastic Teaching Resources

- -

Word Wall Idea: *List compound words, such as* bellboy. *Use the word wall to reinforce the meaning of* compound.

Practice

Sentence With a Compound Predicate

Illustrious Illustration: My pet python took a midtown bus to the museum. My pet python was so famished that he ate three guinea pigs when he got home. **Better:** My pet python took a midtown bus to the museum and was so famished that he ate three guinea pigs when he got home.

Sagacious Suggestion: A *predicate* is the part of a sentence that tells what happened. When the same subject performs two or more actions, you can combine the actions to form a single sentence. Use compound predicates to vary the rhythm and avoid having several short sentences in a row.

Now write your own compound-predicate sentence:

_____

_____

_____

Super Sentences and Perfect Paragraphs © 2009 by Mack Lewis. Scholastic Teaching Resources

- ✂

Super Sentence
Test

Name _____ Date _____

Sentence With a Compound Predicate

Write your own compound-predicate sentence:

_____

_____

_____

_____

Super Sentences and Perfect Paragraphs © 2009 by Mack Lewis. Scholastic Teaching Resources

- -

Word Wall Idea: *List multisyllabic words—words with lots of syllables, such as illustrious— that aren't compounds.*

Name _____   Date _____

Question

Excellence in Action: Why do you always wear your shower cap to the dinner table?

Recurring Reminders: Like all sentences, questions start with a capital letter and end with an ending punctuation mark, in this case, a question mark. Be sure your question includes a word or phrase requiring a response. Some examples are *why, how, do you, what,* and *when.*

Now write your own question:

_____

_____

_____

_____

Super Sentences and Perfect Paragraphs © 2009 by Mack Lewis. Scholastic Teaching Resources

✂

Super Sentence
Test

Name _____   Date _____

Question

Write your own question:

_____

_____

_____

_____

Super Sentences and Perfect Paragraphs © 2009 by Mack Lewis. Scholastic Teaching Resources

Word Wall Idea: *List words or phrases routinely used to start a question, such as* why, how, *and* do you.

Name _____   Date _____

Command

Stunning Sample: Take off your shower cap right now, or I'll feed your liver and onions to the neighbor's goat!

Handy Hint: Commands give orders or directions, but they only require an exclamation point if they're delivered in a commanding tone. For example, at the end of this lesson, your teacher may give you a command requiring only a period: *Turn in your papers.*

Now write your own command:

_____

_____

_____

Super Sentences and Perfect Paragraphs © 2009 by Mack Lewis. Scholastic Teaching Resources

--- ✂ ---

Super Sentence Test

Name _____   Date _____

Command

Write your own command:

_____

_____

_____

_____

Super Sentences and Perfect Paragraphs © 2009 by Mack Lewis. Scholastic Teaching Resources

Word Wall Idea: *List people who give orders, such as* generals, police officers, *and* doggy obedience instructors.

Name _____   Date _____

Practice

Exclamation

Delicious Demonstration: Boy howdy, this sardine sandwich is surprisingly delectable!

Astonishing Advice: Exclamations express emotions such as surprise, glee, and agony. It's sometimes helpful to the reader if the exclamation begins with a word or phrase such as *wow, yikes,* or *boy howdy.*

Now write your own exclamation:

_____

_____

_____

_____

- ✂

Super Sentence
Test

Name _____   Date _____

Exclamation

Write your own exclamation:

_____

_____

_____

_____

- -

Word Wall Idea: *List exclamation words or phrases, such as* wow, yikes, *or for crying out loud.*

Name _____   Date _____

Sentence Containing a Fact

Exemplary Example: According to the *Encyclopedia Britannica,* the common blue jay is one of the smartest birds on the planet.

Radical Rule of Thumb: It's a good idea to begin your sentence with a phrase that tells the readers you're stating a fact, such as *According to studies . . . , Research says . . . ,* or *Studies show. . . .* It's also important to tell where you found your information. Remember to include details, too.

Now write your own fact sentence:

_____

_____

_____

Super Sentence Test

Name _____   Date _____

Sentence Containing a Fact

Write your own fact sentence:

_____

_____

_____

_____

Word Wall Idea: *List sources for finding facts, such as* encyclopedias, magazines, *and* spy documents.

Sentence Expressing an Opinion

Exquisite Exemplar: In my opinion, baby carrots should be banned from our school cafeteria because they haven't yet had the chance to live their full carrot lives.

Resplendent Recommendations: It's a good idea to begin your sentence with a phrase that tells readers you're expressing an opinion, such as *In my opinion . . .* , *I think . . .* , or *I believe. . . .* It's also important to tell why you are of that opinion. Remember to include details, too.

Now write your own opinion sentence:

_____

_____

_____

- ✂

Super Sentence Test

Name _____ Date _____

Sentence Expressing an Opinion

Write your own opinion sentence:

_____

_____

_____

_____

Word Wall Idea: *List parts of books such as* table of contents, chapters, *and* copyright.

Name _____   Date _____

Sentence Pair
(subject sentence and detail sentence)

Profound Prototype: Everyone knows the cheetah is the fastest land mammal, but what I find most fascinating about it is its tail. Without such a long tail, a cheetah wouldn't be able to keep its balance when running so doggone fast!

Neighborly Notes: When you don't have room for the most delectable details in your main sentence, add a detail sentence! This will help you avoid unnecessarily long sentences and run-ons.

Now write your own sentence pair:

_____

_____

_____

Super Sentences and Perfect Paragraphs © 2009 by Mack Lewis. Scholastic Teaching Resources

---

Super Sentence Test

Name _____   Date _____

Sentence Pair
(subject sentence and detail sentence)

Write your own sentence pair:

_____

_____

_____

Super Sentences and Perfect Paragraphs © 2009 by Mack Lewis. Scholastic Teaching Resources

Word Wall Idea: *List antonym pairs, such as* dangerous/safe *and* past/future.

Name _____ Date _____

Sentence Trio
(subject sentence and two detail sentences)

Shining Sample: My birthday cake was a disaster! The frosting was this nasty, bat-guano green, and the flowers looked like melted clown faces. Worst of all, my name was misspelled!

Superlative Suggestion: You can change the rhythm of a piece of writing by including sentences of varying lengths. For example, you can break a compound sentence into a sentence pair or a sentence trio. This also helps make your main sentence clear and to the point.

Now write your own sentence trio:

_____

_____

_____

Super Sentence **Test**

Name _____ Date _____

Sentence Trio
(subject sentence and two detail sentences)

Write your own sentence trio:

_____

_____

_____

Word Wall Idea: *List synonym pairs and trios, such as* simple/easy *and* rich/wealthy/loaded.

Past-Tense Sentence

Magnificent Model: Three days ago, my friend Matthew found a baby alligator happily doing the backstroke in the upstairs bathtub.

Rambunctious Reminders: You can make sure a sentence is written in the past tense by telling when the event happened, with words such as *yesterday* or *last July*. Notice how it is set off by a comma when it appears at the beginning of the sentence. Don't forget those spicy details!

Now write your own past-tense sentence:

_____

_____

_____

✂

Super Sentence Test

Name _____ **Date** _____

Past-Tense Sentence

Write your own past-tense sentence:

_____

_____

_____

_____

Word Wall Idea: *List words or phrases that tell when something happened, such as* yesterday, two days ago, *and* in a minute. *Discuss whether each phrase shows past, present, or future tense.*

Name _____   Date _____

Future-Tense Sentence

Doggone-Good Demonstration: Next month, when the moon is full, I'm going to stay up all night to see what happens after dark.

Heralded Hint: Words and phrases such as *will* and *going to* help establish that the action will happen in the future, which could be as little as a split-second away. As always, remember to include specific details.

Now write your own future-tense sentence:

_____

_____

_____

- ✂

Super Sentence Test

Name _____   Date _____

Future-Tense Sentence

Write your own future-tense sentence:

_____

_____

_____

_____

- -

Word Wall Idea: *List onomatopoeia words such as* meow, bang, *and* splat.

Name _____   Date _____

Present-Tense Sentence

Extravagant Example: Right now I am strapping myself into the Super-Spiral Roller Coaster, but I'm really worried because the guy sitting in front of me said he just ate three chili dogs.

Enthralling Rule of Thumb: You can use phrases such as *right now, at the moment,* and *currently* to indicate that the action is taking place in the present. Imagine you're on a cell phone telling someone what you're doing that instant!

Now write your own present-tense sentence:

_____

_____

_____

✂

Super Sentence Test

Name _____   Date _____

Present-Tense Sentence

Write your own present-tense sentence:

_____

_____

_____

_____

Word Wall Idea: List things that go splat, such as water balloons *and* spitballs.

Name _____   Date _____

Sentence With Commas in a Series

Dashing Demo: One time, at this weird dinner party, my mom made me eat oysters, beef tongue, pickled pig's feet, and seared octopus.

Warmhearted Warning: When you list three or more items within a sentence, it's called a *series*. Put a comma between each item in the list, including before the word *and*.

Now write your own sentence with commas in a series:

_____

_____

_____

_____

Super Sentences and Perfect Paragraphs © 2009 by Mack Lewis. Scholastic Teaching Resources

- ✂

Super Sentence Test

Name _____   Date _____

Sentence With Commas in a Series

Write your own sentence with commas in a series:

_____

_____

_____

_____

Super Sentences and Perfect Paragraphs © 2009 by Mack Lewis. Scholastic Teaching Resources

- -

Word Wall Idea: *List "weird" foods, such as* octopus *and* pig's feet.

Practice

Sentence With a Series as the Subject

Efficient Exemplar: Earlier today Mr. Jones, my Aunt Paulie, and I went to the zoo and saw three hyenas wearing tuxedos.

Reasonable Reminders: A series is a list three or more items in a sentence. Sometimes the subject of a sentence is a series. Remember to put a comma between each item in the list, including before the word *and*. If you're including yourself in the series, put yourself last.

Now write your own sentence with a series as the subject:

_____

_____

_____

- ✂

Super Sentence
Test

Name _____   Date _____

Sentence With a Series as the Subject

Write your own sentence with a series as the subject:

_____

_____

_____

_____

Word Wall Idea: *List common abbreviations (which, other than such exceptions as Mr., Mrs., and Jr., don't belong in formal writing). Also, be sure to distinguish between abbreviations and acronyms.*

Practice

Sentence With a Complex Series

Princely Prototype: When the buzzards attacked my dad's car, they left scratches all over the hood, broke the antenna in two, cracked the windshield, and stole the spare tire.

First-Rate Recommendations: A series—or list of items—need not be limited to single objects; you can also join a list of events, actions, or objects with detailed descriptions. Don't forget to include that comma before the last *and*.

Now write your own sentence with a complex series:

_____

_____

_____

- ✂

Super Sentence
Test

Name _____   Date _____

Sentence With a Complex Series

Write your own sentence with a complex series:

_____

_____

_____

_____

- -

Word Wall Idea: *List acronyms, such as FBI, UCLA, and BFFL. But clarify the difference between acronyms and text-messaging shorthand, and be sure to emphasize that the latter doesn't belong in formal writing.*

Name _____   Date _____

Sentence Using a Colon
to Introduce a List

Intriguing Illustration: I like to put all kinds of yummy stuff on baked potatoes: sweet butter, sour cream, cheddar cheese, bacon bits, sliced olives, green onions, and sometimes even dill pickles.

Auriferous Advice: When your series—or list of items—is going to be lengthy, you can introduce it with a colon. The first part of the sentence should tell what the list is about, and it should be able to stand alone as a sentence if you left off the list.

Now write your own sentence using a colon to introduce a list:

_____

_____

_____

Super Sentence Test

Name _____   Date _____

Sentence Using a Colon
to Introduce a List

Write your own sentence using a colon to introduce a list:

_____

_____

_____

Word Wall Idea: *List common prefixes, such as* un-, hemi-, *and* pre-.

Name _____   Date _____

Sentence Using a Colon
to Show What Follows

Scintillating Specimen: When a bunch of scientists decided Pluto wasn't really a planet, my friend Dave went around screaming like a nincompoop: It seems he thought he'd been born there.

Knock-Out Notes: The colon has many uses, such as to introduce an example or explanation (as in the Scintillating Specimen). Remember, what comes before the colon must be able to stand alone as a sentence.

Now write your own sentence using a colon to show what follows:

_____

_____

_____

- ✂

Super Sentence Test

Name _____   Date _____

Sentence Using a Colon
to Show What Follows

Write your own sentence using a colon to show what follows:

_____

_____

_____

- -

Word Wall Idea: *List common suffixes, such as -ed, -est, and -ing.*

Name _____   Date _____

Sentence Featuring a Simile

Sensible Sample: When he's got the chainsaw in his hands, my older brother acts *as ferocious as a lion* tearing into its prey.

High-Minded Hints: A *simile* is an imaginative way to make a comparison. It shows how two things that are different in most ways are alike in one specific way. When you create similes, use the words *like* or *as* to make the comparison.

Now write your own sentence featuring a simile:

_____

_____

_____

- ✂

Super Sentence Test

Name _____   Date _____

Sentence Featuring a Simile

Write your own sentence featuring a simile:

_____

_____

_____

_____

Word Wall Idea: *List homophone pairs and trios—words that sound the same but have different spellings. For example,* their/there/they're.

Sentence Featuring a Metaphor

Erudite Example: My pet goat is nothing but a garbage disposal on four legs.

Impeccable Ideas: While similes use the words *as* or *like* to make a comparison, *metaphors* simply state that something *is* something else. It's another figure of speech used to make one's writing more interesting and entertaining.

Now write your own sentence featuring a metaphor:

_____

_____

_____

_____

Super Sentences and Perfect Paragraphs © 2009 by Mack Lewis. Scholastic Teaching Resources

- ✂

Super Sentence Test

Name _____   Date _____

Sentence Featuring a Metaphor

Write your own sentence featuring a metaphor:

_____

_____

_____

_____

Super Sentences and Perfect Paragraphs © 2009 by Mack Lewis. Scholastic Teaching Resources

- -

Word Wall Idea: *List homographs—words that have the same spelling but different meanings. For example,* tear, wind, *and* use.

Name _____ Date _____

Rhetorical Question

Mild-Mannered Model: When was the last time you had so much fun you felt like a newborn monkey tasting his first ripe banana?

Sincere Suggestion: A rhetorical question is posed to express a feeling or attitude rather than to receive an answer. Make sure your question creates images that match the feeling you want to portray.

Now write your own rhetorical question:

_____

_____

_____

_____

Super Sentence **Test**

Name _____ Date _____

Rhetorical Question

Write your own rhetorical question:

_____

_____

_____

_____

Word Wall Idea: *List exciting careers, such as botanist, food engineer, or NASCAR spotter.*

Practice

Sentence Containing a Title

Dandy Demo: Roald Dahl wrote many great books, such as *James and the Giant Peach*, but I think some of his best works are his crazy poems, like "Little Red Riding Hood and the Wolf."

Rational Reminder: Use italics or underline to indicate the title of a book, magazine, or film, but use quotation marks to indicate the title of a shorter work, such as an article, song, or poem.

Now write your own sentence containing a title:

_____

_____

_____

_____

Super Sentences and Perfect Paragraphs © 2009 by Mack Lewis. Scholastic Teaching Resources

Super Sentence
Test

Sentence Containing a Title

Write your own sentence containing a title:

_____

_____

_____

_____

Super Sentences and Perfect Paragraphs © 2009 by Mack Lewis. Scholastic Teaching Resources

Word Wall Idea: List things that have titles, such as books, TV shows, and royalty.

Name _____   Date _____

Sentence Containing . . . Ellipses

Promising Prototype: When I was walking through the woods I had this strange feeling something was . . . watching me.

World-Class Warning: Ellipses are formally used to show that words have been left out of a quotation. However, it has become common to use the three dots in a more creative way: to suggest confusion, worry, or a tailing off of your thought. Many people use ellipses too much, so be careful!

Now write your own sentence containing ellipses:

_____

_____

_____

- ✂ - -

Super Sentence Test

Name _____   Date _____

Sentence Containing . . . Ellipses

Write your own sentence containing ellipses:

_____

_____

_____

_____

- -

Word Wall Idea: *List favorite authors, such as* Roald Dahl, Gary Paulsen, *and* Laura Ingalls Wilder.

Name _____ Date _____

Sentence Containing Parentheses

Explicit Exemplar: If pigs could fly, I'd invest my money (if I had any) in a company that makes heavy-duty umbrellas.

Refreshing Recommendations: Parentheses are used to include information that is not essential but perhaps adds color or detail. Be sure your sentence would still be meaningful if the information in the parentheses was left out.

Now write your own sentence containing parentheses:

_____

_____

_____

Super Sentences and Perfect Paragraphs © 2009 by Mack Lewis. Scholastic Teaching Resources

- ✂

Super Sentence Test

Name _____ Date _____

Sentence Containing Parentheses

Write your own sentence containing parentheses:

_____

_____

_____

_____

Super Sentences and Perfect Paragraphs © 2009 by Mack Lewis. Scholastic Teaching Resources

- -

Word Wall Idea: *List weather words, such as* wind, rain, *and* climatologist.

Name _____   Date _____

Cause-and-Effect Sentence

Dapper Demonstration: Because temperatures on the planet are getting warmer, weather patterns are less predictable.

Rhapsodic Rule of Thumb: Here's your chance to start a sentence with *because*! Place similar words or phrases such as *since, as a result of,* and *due to* in front of the reason something happens. The reason is the *cause*, and what happens is the *effect*. In this case, the changing temperatures are the cause of less predictable weather patterns, the effect.

Now write your own cause-and-effect sentence:

_____

_____

_____

Super Sentence Test

Name _____   Date _____

Cause-and-Effect Sentence

Write your own cause-and-effect sentence:

_____

_____

_____

_____

Word Wall Idea: *List words describing Earth, such as* spherical, habitable, *and* rocky.

If/Then Sentence

Space-Age Specimen: If the moon were made of cheese, the space shuttle would have a serious rat problem.

Irrefutable Ideas: The if/then form is called a *conditional sentence*. It shows the consequences of a given event. Start your sentence with *if*. Use *then* to start the part of the sentence containing the consequence. Often, the word *then* can be left out, as it was in the Space-Age Specimen.

Now write your own if/then sentence:

_____

_____

_____

- ✂

Super Sentence Test

Name _____   Date _____

If/Then Sentence

Write your own if/then sentence:

_____

_____

_____

_____

- -

Word Wall Idea: List words having to do with space or the cosmos.

Name _____   Date _____

Sentence With a Subordinate Clause

Iconic Illustration: My friend Ahmad, who led the campaign to boycott cafeteria food, just got a job at a fast food place.

Transcendent Thought: A *subordinate clause* gives extra information about something in the sentence. It normally starts with the word *who*, *whom*, *which*, *whose*, and *that*. Put commas at the beginning and end of the clause to set it apart from the main idea.

Now write your own sentence with a subordinate clause:

_____

_____

_____

- ✂

Super Sentence Test

Name _____   Date _____

Sentence With a Subordinate Clause

Write your own sentence with a subordinate clause:

_____

_____

_____

_____

Word Wall Idea: *List challenge words—the toughest words your students can find, such as floccinaucinihilipilification.*

Name _____ Date _____

Sentence Using Dashes
to Set Off a Point

Sanctioned Sample: On my new cell phone—which cost me an entire year's allowance—I can take pictures, stream video, send text, and even place calls.

Humdinger of a Hint: The dash is a stronger version of the comma (as well as a stronger form of parentheses). It's used to *emphasize* information within a sentence. Note that when you remove the clause created by the dash or dashes, the sentence must still be able to stand alone. Also, don't confuse the dash with the hyphen, which is used with certain compound words.

Now write your own sentence using dashes to set off a point:

_____

_____

- ✂

Super Sentence Test

Name _____ Date _____

Sentence Using Dashes
to Set Off a Point

Write your own sentence using dashes to set off a point:

_____

_____

_____

- -

Word Wall Idea: *List things that have points, such as* pencils, peninsulas, *and* stories.

Practice

Detailed Simple Sentence

Made-to-Order Model: The band of penguins squealed in unison when they escaped from their pen and swarmed the churros stand.

Well-Seasoned Suggestions: Add detail by including one or more of the "Five W's": *who, what, where, when,* and *why.* Don't forget to double-check your capitals and end marks!

Now write your own detailed sentence:

_____

_____

_____

_____

✂

Super Sentence
Test

Name _____   Date _____

Detailed Simple Sentence

Write your own detailed sentence:

_____

_____

_____

_____

Word Wall Idea: *List sentence-writing tools, such as* commas, dashes, *and* metaphors.

Name _____   Date _____

Super Sentence of Your Choice

Yet Another Example: As she peered into the high-powered microscope, Shannon groaned, "Ooh, there are tiny little parasites living under my fingernails!"

Hints Worth Hearing Again: Whether commas, quotation marks, or simple end marks, remember to double-check that you've used your sentence-writing tools correctly.

Now write your own super sentence:

_____

_____

_____

_____

Super Sentences and Perfect Paragraphs © 2009 by Mack Lewis. Scholastic Teaching Resources

- ✂

Super Sentence Test

Name _____   Date _____

Super Sentence of Your Choice

Write your own super sentence:

_____

_____

_____

_____

Super Sentences and Perfect Paragraphs © 2009 by Mack Lewis. Scholastic Teaching Resources

- -

Word Wall Idea: *List vacation words.*

The Verbose Sentence

Slick Specimen: Three weeks ago last Tuesday at the San Luis Obispo Zoo, the normally meek band of white-flippered penguins finally became disenchanted with their strict diet of dead fish and Purina-brand zoo chow, with the taunts of little children singing, "I scream for ice cream," and the unceasing laughter from the hyena enclosure (the penguins were sure the laughter was directed at them), so with complete disregard for the day's immense heat and the rent-a-cops who regularly patrol the zoo grounds, the penguins rose up as a species to escape their confines and, while squealing in unison, swarmed the variety of vendors stationed around the zoo: the hot-dog man, the snow-cone machine, the gyro stand, the licorice-whip guy, the helium-balloon salesman (who for some unknown reason befuddled the penguins), the waffle-cone booth, and, last but not least, the churros cart, with which the penguins seemed particularly enthralled—only to be in the end found sprawled upon the sidewalk near the polar bear exhibit clutching their tiny arctic tummies and chirping something incoherent that the zookeepers took to mean, "Please forgive us our folly, return us to our home, and get us some Pepto Bismol *tout de suite*" . . . which is just what the zookeepers did.

Super Sentences and Perfect Paragraphs © 2009 by Mack Lewis. Scholastic Teaching Resources

Cheerful Challenge: Although lengthy sentences are often frowned upon, if you correctly use all your sentence tools—colons, semicolons, dashes, ellipses, parentheses, quotation marks, and the rest—you can create a truly super sentence, a single sentence that tells a story all by itself. Are you up to the challenge?

Now write your own super sentence:

_____

_____

_____

_____

_____

(Continue your sentence on the back.)

Super Sentences and Perfect Paragraphs © 2009 by Mack Lewis. Scholastic Teaching Resources

Name _____   Date _____

Basic Paragraph Paste-Up
Descriptive
My Crazy Cat

Directions: The sentences below fit together to form a Perfect Paragraph, but they're all mixed up. Cut them out and paste them in the correct order using Paragraph Template #1 (page 89) to form a great descriptive paragraph. When finished, try writing your own Perfect Paragraph describing a favorite pet you have or would like to have.

When he's ready to pounce, they're as big as dimes.

Another reason I like him is that he has crazy eyes.

One reason I like him is because he's athletic.

My favorite pet is my cat, Buckley.

Cats like Buckley make life more enjoyable.

Yesterday he climbed the screen door all the way to the ceiling.

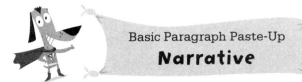

Basic Paragraph Paste-Up
Narrative

A Vacation Memory

Directions: The sentences below fit together to form a Perfect Paragraph, but they're all mixed up. Cut them out and paste them in the correct order using Paragraph Template #1 (page 89) to form a great narrative paragraph. When finished, try writing your own Perfect Paragraph about something you did during your vacation from school.

It turns out strawberries aren't so great for baking.

It was wonderful having pie, but it was even better making it with my friends.

We picked the berries behind the house.

This summer, Shelby and Cali came to my house and helped me bake a blackberry pie.

We used the leftover dough to make a strawberry tart.

Shelby ate more than she put in the bucket.

Name _____   Date _____

Basic Paragraph Paste-Up
Expository

Killer Snake

Directions: The sentences below fit together to form a Perfect Paragraph, but they're all mixed up. Cut them out and paste them in the correct order using Paragraph Template #1 (page 89) to form a great expository paragraph. When finished, try writing your own Perfect Paragraph about a creature you find fascinating.

It is one of the deadliest snakes in the world.

In his book, *Going Solo*, Roald Dahl writes about the mamba.

The black mamba is a fascinating species of snake.

He tells how a mamba attacks his African gardener.

I hope I never meet a mamba.

Its venom is five times as poisonous as that of the king cobra.

Name _____   Date _____

Basic Paragraph Paste-Up
Imaginative

Horatio the Hornet

Directions: The sentences below fit together to form a Perfect Paragraph, but they're all mixed up. Cut them out and paste them in the correct order using Paragraph Template #1 (page 89) to form a great imaginative paragraph. When finished, try making up your own silly short story using the Perfect Paragraph formula.

Suddenly, a giant blue net lifted him from the water
and set him on solid ground.

From then on, Horatio was one of the best pollinators around—
but he was a lot more careful about where he went to cool off.

At first, the tiny droplets of water felt refreshing, but then
his left wing caught a wave, and he was pulled in.

He heard a voice say, "These days we need all the
pollinators we can get—even hornets."

Horatio the Hornet was getting overheated, so he tried
to skim the surface of a swimming pool to get a drink.

Now all the water felt cold and heavy, and
Horatio knew he was doomed.

Super Sentences and Perfect Paragraphs © 2009 by Mack Lewis. Scholastic Teaching Resources

Basic Paragraph Paste-Up
Persuasive

No More Broccoli

Directions: The sentences below fit together to form a Perfect Paragraph, but they're all mixed up. Cut them out and paste them in the correct order using Paragraph Template #1 (page 89) to form a great persuasive paragraph. When finished, try writing your own Perfect Paragraph about a change you'd like to see in your school cafeteria.

Secondly, it's good for you.

That's why I think we should replace broccoli with something kids actually want, like powdered donuts.

There are some good reasons broccoli should be banned from the school cafeteria.

What kid wants to eat anything that's nutritious?

The last time I tried some, I started chirping like a squirrel.

First, broccoli may look like cute little trees, but it tastes like tree bark.

Basic Paragraph Paste-Up
Book Review

Diary of a Spider

Directions: The sentences below fit together to form a Perfect Paragraph, but they're all mixed up. Cut them out and paste them in the correct order using Paragraph Template #1 (page 89) to form a well-written book review. When finished, try writing your own Perfect Paragraph reviewing one of your favorite picture books.

It tells what life is like for a spider, with a twist.

Diary of a Spider by Doreen Cronin is one of those hysterically funny picture books kids of any age can enjoy.

They were taught to Stop, Drop, and Run!

This book will make you laugh out loud every time you read it.

My favorite part is when the spiders had a vacuum drill at school.

For example, spiders and flies aren't supposed to get along, but in this book, they're best friends.

Basic Paragraph Rewrite
Descriptive

Thankful

Directions: Unscramble the sentences so that they form a Perfect Paragraph. When finished, color code the sentences as follows: yellow = topic sentence, blue = supporting sentences (each telling something to be thankful for), green = detail sentences, red = concluding sentence.

- First of all, I'm thankful for my miniature poodle, Petunia.
- I'm also thankful for my BMX bike.
- When you count your blessings like this, it's easy to feel happy.
- I'm thankful for many things.
- She plays with me after school and protects me all night.
- Without it, I wouldn't be able to ride to the store to buy Ding Dongs.

_____

_____

_____

_____

_____

_____

_____

_____

_____

Now use the Perfect Paragraph Template #1 (page 89) to write your own paragraph describing things for which you're thankful.

Basic Paragraph Rewrite
Narrative

The Worst Sick Day Ever

Directions: Unscramble the sentences so that they form a Perfect Paragraph. When finished, color code the sentences as follows: yellow = topic sentence, blue = supporting sentences (each telling an event in the story), green = detail sentences, red = concluding sentence.

- My mom took me out of school and drove me to Doctor Bob's office.

- He said I had chicken pox, so I had to rub this slimy stuff all over my body.

- I must have scratched for ten days straight, which is pretty awful, if you ask me.

- I was at school when little itchy bumps started popping up all over my body.

- My worst sick day ever was when I was in second grade.

- My friend Katy started telling everyone I had zits.

_____

_____

_____

_____

_____

_____

_____

_____

_____

Now use the Perfect Paragraph Template #1 (page 89) to write your own narrative paragraph telling about a time you were sick, real or imagined.

Super Sentences and Perfect Paragraphs © 2009 by Mack Lewis. Scholastic Teaching Resources

Name _____ Date _____

Basic Paragraph Rewrite
Expository

How to Make a Sandwich

Directions: Unscramble the sentences so that they form a Perfect Paragraph. When finished, color code the sentences as follows: yellow = topic sentence, blue = supporting sentences (each telling one of the steps), green = detail sentences, red = concluding sentence.

- It's pretty messy, so be prepared to do some washing up.

- There are probably more steps than that, but come on—who can't make a sandwich?

- Next, you stuff it in your mouth.

- You can use marmalade instead of jelly, but I wouldn't recommend it.

- Here's how to make a great peanut butter and jelly sandwich.

- The first thing you do is take out some bread and slap on some PB and J.

_____

_____

_____

_____

_____

_____

_____

_____

_____

Now use the Perfect Paragraph Template #1 (page 89) to write your own "how-to" paragraph explaining how to do a simple task.

Basic Paragraph Rewrite
Imaginative

A Quick Trip to Mars

Directions: Unscramble the sentences so that they form a Perfect Paragraph. When finished, color code the sentences as follows: yellow = topic sentence, blue = supporting sentences (each telling an event in the story), green = detail sentences, red = concluding sentence.

- The landing was a bit rough, but the garbage-can lid protected us.

- Believe it or not, my best friend, Justin, built a spaceship out of a garbage can, a lawn-mower engine, and a box of dynamite he found in his dad's shop.

- After looking around for a while, we found a Martian building a spaceship of his own.

- He flew us back to Earth just in time for science class.

- It was a lot fancier than ours.

- We blasted into space and landed on Mars.

_____

_____

_____

_____

_____

_____

_____

_____

Now use the Perfect Paragraph Template #1 (page 89) to write your own imaginative story about your space adventure.

Name _____   Date _____

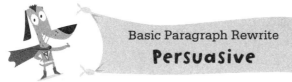

Basic Paragraph Rewrite
Persuasive
More Time Outside

Directions: Unscramble the sentences so that they form a Perfect Paragraph. When finished, color code the sentences as follows: yellow = topic sentence, blue = supporting sentences (each giving a reason why the topic sentence is true), green = detail sentences, red = concluding sentence.

- First of all, experts say kids need more fresh air and exercise.
- I have a friend who got so sick of grammar lessons, he started chewing a hole in his desk!
- How are we going to get it if we never see the sun?
- I believe kids need to spend more time outside.
- Like all kids, he needs to get outdoors more often.
- Secondly, kids get a little crazy doing schoolwork all the time.

_____

_____

_____

_____

_____

_____

_____

_____

What's your opinion? Use the Perfect Paragraph Template #1 (page 89) to write your own persuasive paragraph explaining why kids should spend more (or less) time outside (or inside).

Basic Paragraph Rewrite
Book Review
Runny Babbit

Directions: Unscramble the sentences so that they form a Perfect Paragraph book review. When finished, color code the sentences as follows: yellow = topic sentence, blue = supporting sentences, green = detail sentences, red = concluding sentence. Supporting sentences sometimes explain what makes the book enjoyable and sometimes tell about an important or favorite event in the story.

- It's about a group of animals that say things in a different sort of way.

- So if you'd like to bead a great rook, try *Runny Babbit*!

- *Runny Babbit* is another silly book of poetry by Shel Silverstein.

- One of my favorite poems in the book is "Runny's Mancy Feal."

- The waiter offers him crazy things like fickled pish and suna talad, but all Runny asks for is one caw rarrot.

- They swap the first letter of key words, yet once you learn the lingo, the poems make sense.

_____

_____

_____

_____

_____

_____

_____

Now use the Perfect Paragraph Template #1 (page 89) to write your own review of a favorite book.

My Survival Crate

Directions: The sentences below fit together to form a Perfect Paragraph, but they're all mixed up. Cut them out and paste them in the correct order using Paragraph Template #2 (page 90). Be careful—one sentence doesn't belong! When finished, color code the sentences as follows: yellow = topic sentence, blue = supporting sentences (each identifying an item in the crate), green = detail sentences, and red = concluding sentence.

Next, I'd bring a harmonica.	I've always wanted to learn it, and with a month at sea, I'd have plenty of time.
Finally, I'd be sure to bring some long underwear.	I have a feeling the sailors get a bit hungry on those trips.
I also want to learn how to play the electric guitar.	First of all, I would bring a secret stash of beef jerky.
If I had all that stuff, I might just make it.	Two pairs would be even better.
If I were sailing across the Atlantic with Columbus, I would pack my crate very carefully.	

Now use the Perfect Paragraph Template #2 to write your own paragraph describing the things you would pack in one small crate on your journey across the ocean with Amerigo Vespucci or some other explorer, or across China with Marco Polo, or to Oregon on the Overland Trail.

Name _____   Date _____

River Kayaks

Directions: The sentences below fit together to form a Perfect Paragraph, but they're all mixed up. Cut them out and paste them in the correct order using Paragraph Template #2 (page 90). Be careful—one sentence doesn't belong! When finished, color code the sentences as follows: yellow = topic sentence, blue = supporting sentences (each identifying an event in the narrative), green = detail sentences, and red = concluding sentence.

At first, the river was slow and calm, which was great for spotting wildlife.	We rented kayaks and put in at a place called Graves Creek.
Pretty soon, the river started running wild.	Last summer, I had a great time kayaking down the river.
The kayaks looked a little like torpedoes.	I thought the rapids would swallow me alive.
That was an outdoor adventure I'll never forget.	I saw a bald eagle make off with a fish, and three deer standing on a sandbar.
We had a big taco dinner when we got home.	

Now use the Perfect Paragraph Template #2 to write your own narrative paragraph telling about something that happened to you out of doors. It could be about a camping or boating trip, or about something that happened in the backyard or park. It's up to you!

Bully for Teddy Roosevelt

Intermediate Paragraph Paste-Up
Expository

Directions: The sentences below fit together to form a Perfect Paragraph, but they're all mixed up. Cut them out and paste them in the correct order using Paragraph Template #2 (page 90). Be careful—one sentence doesn't belong! When finished, color code the sentences as follows: yellow = topic sentence, blue = supporting sentences (each giving a reason the topic sentence is true), green = detail sentences, and red = concluding sentence.

He's famous for leading the charge up San Juan Hill during the Spanish-American War, but did you know he also saved football?

Theodore Roosevelt is one of the most fascinating people in American history.

He refused to shoot a captured bear during a hunting trip, and all of America cheered him for it.

He helped make the sport safer so that it would not be banned.

There is a lot more to know about Theodore Roosevelt, but it's already easy to see why his face is carved on Mount Rushmore.

Another president I really like is Thomas Jefferson.

Finally, the Teddy Bear is named after Roosevelt.

While president, he created the National Forest system and preserved more than 200 million acres of land, including much of the Grand Canyon.

In addition to sports, he also loved the outdoors and worked hard to protect nature.

Now use the Perfect Paragraph Template #2 to write your own expository paragraph about a famous person in history.

Name _____ Date _____

Inside My Video Game!

Directions: The sentences below fit together to form a Perfect Paragraph, but they're all mixed up. Cut them out and paste them in the correct order using Paragraph Template #2 (page 90). Be careful—one sentence doesn't belong! When finished, color code the sentences as follows: yellow = topic sentence, blue = supporting sentences (each identifying an event in the story), green = detail sentences, and red = concluding sentence.

On Saturday, I was playing my PS2 when somehow I got sucked into Need for Speed, the video game.	I punched the NOS switch and blasted my way across the gap.
It was blue with green flames on the side, and it had a massive Nitrous Oxide System in back.	You can also play Need for Speed on your computer.
Green flames came bursting out of my tailpipe as I flew through the air.	The car I was racing skidded out in front of me, so I hung a quick left.
It was quite a ride, and when I woke up on the sofa, I was all sweaty.	I was ripping through San Francisco in a supercharged Mustang.
The turn sent me heading toward a drawbridge that was opening.	

Now use the Perfect Paragraph Template #2 to write your own imaginative paragraph telling about being stuck inside your favorite video game or TV show.

Vote for Me!

Intermediate Paragraph Paste-Up
Persuasive

Directions: The sentences below fit together to form a Perfect Paragraph, but they're all mixed up. Cut them out and paste them in the correct order using Paragraph Template #2. Be careful—one sentence doesn't belong! When finished, color code your sentences as follows: yellow = topic sentence, blue = supporting sentences (each identifying a reason to vote for you), green = detail sentences, and red = concluding sentence.

When our class wants to make big changes, I'll be willing to meet with him myself.	I think I should be our next class president.
Another good reason to elect me is that I'm not afraid to talk to the principal.	So vote for me, the good-listening, principal-talking, donut-bringing candidate!
He always wears a suit and tie.	Glazed, chocolate-covered, powdered, those ones with all the sprinkles on them—you'll have your choice!
Lastly, I'll bring donuts to class once a month.	First of all, I'm a good listener.
When my friends come to me with their complaints, I always pay attention.	

Now use the Perfect Paragraph Template #2 to write your own persuasive paragraph convincing your classmates to vote for you for class president, student council, team captain, or some other position.

Holes

Directions: The sentences below fit together to form a Perfect Paragraph, but they're all mixed up. Cut them out and paste them in the correct order using Paragraph Template #2 (page 90). Be careful— one sentence doesn't belong! When finished, color code the sentences as follows: yellow = topic sentence, blue = supporting sentences (each giving a reason you liked or didn't like the movie), green = detail sentences, and red = concluding sentence.

One reason I liked the movie is that it follows the book's story line almost exactly.	It's not as good as the book, but I give this flick two thumbs up!
There is no such thing as the yellow-spotted lizard.	It stars Shia LaBeouf as Stanley Yelnats.
He's not quite what I imagined Stanley would look like, but he does a great job with the part.	Another reason is that the bad guys are all so nasty.
If you haven't seen *Holes*, the movie, you've been cheated!	I think that's because Louis Sachar, the author, is also the screenwriter.
The Warden, Mr. Sir, and Mr. Pendanski are all perfectly cast.	

Now use the Perfect Paragraph Template #2 to write your own paragraph reviewing a movie, television show, or music CD.

Intermediate Paragraph Rewrite
Descriptive

The Coolest Room

Directions: Unscramble the sentences so that they form a Perfect Paragraph. When finished, color code the sentences as follows: yellow = topic sentence, blue = supporting sentences (each giving a reason why the topic sentence is true), green = detail sentences, red = concluding sentence.

- Finally, my bunk bed is like a jungle gym.
- I also have a cage full of gerbils.
- My room is special to me because it's full of fantastic sights and sounds.
- Sometimes I pretend I'm a monkey swinging from bunk to bunk.
- When I'm lying in bed, I imagine myself body slamming Stone Cold Steve Austin.
- At night, it's comforting to hear them scratching in the sawdust and shredded paper.
- For one thing, I have lots of wrestling posters tacked to my ceiling.
- I guess I'm pretty lucky to have such a cool room.

_____

_____

_____

_____

_____

_____

_____

_____

_____

Now use the Perfect Paragraph Template #2 (page 90) to write your own paragraph describing your room or some other place that's special to you.

Name _____   Date _____

Intermediate Paragraph Rewrite
Narrative

A Lame Halloween

Directions: Unscramble the sentences so that they form a Perfect Paragraph. When finished, color code the sentences as follows: yellow = topic sentence, blue = supporting sentences (each telling an event in the story), green = detail sentences, red = concluding sentence.

- Finally, when I went trick-or-treating at the mall, all they gave out were three-year-old Tootsie Rolls.

- He made us watch a movie about brushing our teeth instead.

- First of all, my mom made me go to school wearing the same Pokemon costume I wore last year.

- This year, I had the lamest Halloween ever.

- Yep, it was definitely a holiday worth forgetting.

- I cracked a tooth when I tried to chew one.

- The kids all laughed at me when they saw the silly yellow fur and the big, round eyes.

- Next, the teacher cancelled the class party.

_____

_____

_____

_____

_____

_____

_____

_____

_____

Now use the Perfect Paragraph Template #2 (page 90) to write your own narrative paragraph about a holiday event, real or imagined.

Name _____   Date _____

An Important Event in History

Directions: Unscramble the sentences so that they form a Perfect Paragraph. When finished, color code the sentences as follows: yellow = topic sentence, blue = supporting sentences (each telling a fact about the event or why it was important), green = detail sentences, red = concluding sentence.

- It was a huge best-seller, and after reading it, many people started calling for the abolition of slavery.

- It was important because it showed the country what slavery was really like.

- When Lincoln met Stowe, he said, "So you're the little lady that started this great big war."

- A great moment in history was when Harriet Beecher Stowe wrote *Uncle Tom's Cabin*.

- Imagine how different our country might be had she never written those words!

- Stowe's book also shows how important it is to be able to write well.

- It may even have convinced President Abraham Lincoln to fight.

- Through her words, she helped end slavery.

_____

_____

_____

_____

_____

_____

_____

_____

_____

Now use the Perfect Paragraph Template #2 (page 90) to write your own expository paragraph about an event in history. It could be as significant as Pearl Harbor or as trivial as the invention of the paper clip. Gather your facts and use the power of your words!

Name _____   Date _____

Intermediate Paragraph Rewrite
Imaginative

The Day I Met Elvis

Directions: Unscramble the sentences so that they form a Perfect Paragraph. When finished, color code the sentences as follows: yellow = topic sentence, blue = supporting sentences (each telling an event in the story), green = detail sentences, red = concluding sentence.

- To this day, I wonder if he ever caught anything with my jig.

- He introduced himself, and then he asked me what kind of bait I was using.

- He seemed particularly taken with my willowspoon jig, so I let him have it.

- "I just been layin' low" is all he said, and then he paddled away.

- I was fishing for walleye on a lake outside of town when Elvis Presley came rowing up in a canoe.

- It was eerie hearing him say his name in that famous Southern drawl.

- I asked him where he'd been all these years.

- I told him I was using a lure, and I showed him my collection.

_____

_____

_____

_____

_____

_____

_____

_____

_____

Now use the Perfect Paragraph Template #2 (page 90) to write your own imaginative story about a time you met someone famous.

Super Sentences and Perfect Paragraphs © 2009 by Mack Lewis. Scholastic Teaching Resources

Name _____   Date _____

An Energizing Breakfast

Directions: Unscramble the sentences so that they form a Perfect Paragraph. When finished, color code the sentences as follows: yellow = topic sentence, blue = supporting sentences (each giving a reason why the topic sentence is true), green = detail sentences, red = concluding sentence.

- I never need a snack when I have bacon with breakfast.
- One time, I skipped breakfast and then fell asleep during a spelling test!
- I think breakfast is the most important meal of the day.
- There are lots of reasons to eat breakfast.
- First of all, a good breakfast gives you lots of energy.
- Finally, a good breakfast keeps me from getting hungry during class.
- A good breakfast also builds strong bones.
- I always have milk in the morning, which gives me calcium.

_____

_____

_____

_____

_____

_____

_____

_____

_____

_____

Now use the Perfect Paragraph Template #2 (page 90) to write your own persuasive paragraph about good nutrition.

Name _____ Date _____

Intermediate Paragraph Rewrite
Book Review

Boy

Directions: Unscramble the sentences so that they form a Perfect Paragraph. When finished, color code the sentences as follows: yellow = topic sentence, blue = supporting sentences, green = detail sentences, red = concluding sentence. Supporting sentences sometimes explain what makes the book enjoyable and sometimes tell about an important event in the story.

- The store's owner almost has a heart attack, but Roald's punishment is even worse.
- Finally, there's also the tale about how Roald and his friends put a dead mouse in the Gobstopper jar.
- I like this book because you're never sure what's going to happen next.
- In another story, the Matron pours soap in the mouth of a snoring boy.
- When you read *Boy*, which is about Roald Dahl's childhood in boarding school, you see where he got a lot of the ideas for his books.
- This is a hilarious book that makes you glad you don't go to boarding school!
- The Matron reminds me of the Trunchbull in *Matilda*.
- For instance, when Roald gets most of his nose cut off, I almost fell out of my chair!

_____

_____

_____

_____

_____

_____

_____

Now use the Perfect Paragraph Template #2 (page 90)
to write your own review of a favorite book.

Cell Phone Fever

Directions: Unscramble the sentences so that they form a
Perfect Paragraph. When finished, color code the sentences as follows: yellow = topic sentence,
blue = supporting sentences (each identifying one of the phone's features), green = detail sentences,
red = concluding sentence. The first sentence has been written for you.

- Lastly, it has text messaging in 18 languages.
- It would be even better if I could figure out how to place a call, but with all these other great features to keep me busy, who has time to talk on the phone anyway?
- Yesterday, I watched YouTube until my battery died!
- My cell phone also has GPS, which means my friends can track me down anywhere on earth.
- Nothing drives my friends crazier than when I text them in Chinese.
- It does all the usual stuff, but it also downloads videos from the Internet at the touch of a button.
- How I'd end up in Siberia is anybody's guess.
- The best video was about a girl whose cell phone overheated and caught her purse on fire.
- If I ever get lost in Siberia, somebody will be able to find me.
- Half the time I don't know what I'm saying to them, but my cell phone seems to.

I just got the best cell phone ever! _____

_____

_____

_____

_____

_____

_____

_____

_____

_____

Now use the Perfect Paragraph Template #3 (page 91) to write your own
paragraph describing an exciting new techno-gadget, real or imagined.

My First Date

Directions: Unscramble the sentences so that they form a Perfect Paragraph. When finished, color code the sentences as follows: yellow = topic sentence, blue = supporting sentences (each identifying an event), green = detail sentences, red = concluding sentence. The first sentence has been written for you.

- I thought the story was really stupid, but Alvin was practically rolling around in the aisle laughing hysterically!
- I guess that's what you get when you mess around with boys.
- It's about how all Gilligan's grandkids get shipwrecked.
- After he had scarfed down his second Big Mac, I noticed he had something disgusting stuck between his teeth.
- First, his mom drove us to the movie theater so we could see *Gilligan's Island: The Next Generation.*
- Next, Alvin took me to lunch at the McDonald's across the street.
- It made me sick, and now that's all I can think about when I look at Alvin.

On Saturday, I went on a date with my new boyfriend, Alvin.

_____

_____

_____

_____

_____

_____

_____

_____

_____

Now use the Perfect Paragraph Template #3 (page 91) to write your own paragraph telling about a first event in your life that turned out badly.

Name _____   Date _____

Homemade Soup
From a Can

Directions: Unscramble the sentences so that
they form a Perfect Paragraph. When finished, color code the sentences as follows: yellow = topic
sentence, blue = supporting sentences (each telling one of the steps), green = detail sentences,
red = concluding sentence. The first sentence has been written for you.

- Next, you pour the soup into a bowl.
- Finally, you take it out and chow down.
- Some microwave ovens have one button that says "soup."
- I just love Chicken With Stars.
- After that, you put it in the microwave and press a few buttons.
- First, you open the can.
- I look for cans with pop-tops so that I don't have to use a can opener.
- Okay, maybe it isn't really homemade, but it tastes great and it's easy to fix!
- You should make sure the bowl is safe for the microwave.

Making homemade soup is easy if you know the steps.

_____

_____

_____

_____

_____

_____

_____

_____

_____

Now use the Perfect Paragraph Template #3 (page 91) to write your own
expository paragraph telling about how to make a special meal.

Name _____ Date _____

Why I Invented the Phlurg

Directions: Unscramble the sentences so that they form a Perfect Paragraph. When finished, color code the sentences as follows: yellow = topic sentence, blue = supporting sentences (each telling something about the invention), green = detail sentences, red = concluding sentence. The first sentence has been written for you.

- It injects freshness into the gum so that when you go to munch on it again, it still tastes great.
- Check out the Phlurg at select retailers everywhere!
- That way you can safely hide it in your pocket before anyone is the wiser.
- When the playground monitor starts looking at you funny, you can turn away and slip your gum into the Phlurg.
- One big benefit is that it will keep you out of trouble.
- Instead of sticking your wad under your desk or tossing it on the sidewalk, you can store it in your Phlurg.
- The Phlurg also helps keep the planet green.
- The Phlurg is a container you can put your gum in when you're not chewing it.

Hasbro has just paid me over a million dollars for my newest invention, the Phlurg.

_____

_____

_____

_____

_____

_____

_____

_____

Now use the Perfect Paragraph Template #3 (page 91) to write your own imaginative paragraph telling about a crazy invention you've created.

Name _____   Date _____

Reasons for a Water Bottle

Directions: Unscramble the sentences so that they form a Perfect Paragraph. When finished, color code the sentences as follows: yellow = topic sentence, blue = supporting sentences (each giving a reason the topic sentence is true), green = detail sentences, red = concluding sentence. The first sentence has been written for you.

- One time, I drank too much of it, and it made me sick.
- Be careful, though, because that could land you in the principal's office.
- Finally, if somebody's bugging you, you can bop him on the head or squirt him in the eye.
- Also, having your own water bottle means you don't have to get up to get a drink.
- For one thing, it means you don't have to drink the nasty stuff coming out of the school's rusty pipes.
- Why go through all that trouble just because you're thirsty?
- I think having a water bottle is a good idea.
- The nurse made me drink half a bottle of Pepto Bismol!

There are lots of reasons to bring your own water bottle to school.

_____

_____

_____

_____

_____

_____

_____

_____

Now use the Perfect Paragraph Template #3 (page 91) to write your own persuasive paragraph convincing your classmates about an idea of yours.

Name _____   Date _____

Harris and Me

Directions: Unscramble the sentences so that they form a Perfect Paragraph book review. When finished, color code the sentences as follows: yellow = topic sentence, blue = supporting sentences (each giving a reason you liked or disliked the book), green = detail sentences, red = concluding sentence. The first sentence has been written for you.

- He lands on a pig and gets attacked by his family's evil rooster, Ernie.
- You should read it!
- I like this book because you never know what Harris is going to do next.
- His overalls got torn off him in the crash!
- In another chapter, Harris pretends he's Tarzan and jumps out of the hayloft.
- Whenever Harris cusses—which he does a lot—she smacks him upside the head.
- The book is also full of great characters, such as Harris's sister, Glennis.
- This book is a scream and makes you wish you were related to a "gooner" like Harris!
- When he hooked a washing-machine motor to a bicycle, I laughed my head off.

Harris and Me by Gary Paulsen is totally crazy! _____

_____

_____

_____

_____

_____

_____

_____

_____

Now use the Perfect Paragraph Template #3 (page 91) to write your own book review about a chapter book you liked or disliked.

Name _____   Date _____

Multi-Paragraph Project
Descriptive

All About Me

Directions: Use the guidelines shown here and on the Perfect Paragraph Template #4 (page 92) to write an essay describing yourself. Prewrite, edit, revise, and draft a final copy.

Introduction *(3- to 5-sentence topic paragraph)*

Introduce yourself. Tell one or two things that make you unique. Are you unusually fast? Do you dress in interesting ways? Can you eat a whole handful of jalapeño peppers in one go?

Background *(5- to 8-sentence paragraph)*

Tell about your family and where you're from. Do you have a sibling to whom you're especially close? Have you lived in the same place all your life, or were you born somewhere else? What's it like hanging out with your family?

Changes *(5- to 8-sentence paragraph)*

If you could change something about yourself, what would it be and why? Are you too short to reach the cookie jar? Does your grandmother call you her "little freckle face"?

Growing Up *(5- to 8-sentence paragraph)*

What do you want to do when you grow up? Travel around the world? Be in a rock band? Become an anthropologist? Why?

Name _____ Date _____

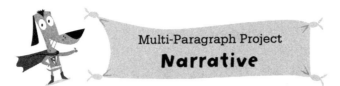

Multi-Paragraph Project
Narrative

Family Vacation

Directions: Use the guidelines shown here and on the Perfect Paragraph Template #4 (page 92) to write a narrative telling about a big trip you went on. Perhaps you flew to Disney World or took the train to Coney Island or went hiking in the Rockies. If you haven't been on a big trip, write about the trip you'd like to go on. Prewrite, edit, revise, and draft a final copy.

Introduction *(3- to 5-sentence topic paragraph)*
Introduce the topic with an opinion about what a great (or lousy) time you had on the trip. Don't forget to say where you went.

Travel *(5- to 8-sentence paragraph)*
Tell how you got there and with whom you were traveling. Did anything odd or interesting happen on the way? Tell how you felt as you got closer to your destination.

The Destination *(5- to 8-sentence paragraph)*
Tell what you did while you were there. Try to hit on different senses: the sights, the sounds, the feel of the wind against your face. Avoid sentences like "It was fun," and instead show emotions and feelings with action: "We screamed hysterically when the roller coaster did the loop-the-loop."

Reflect *(5- to 8-sentence paragraph)*
Tell or show how you felt as the trip came to an end. Would you want to go there again? Why? Are you looking forward to your next family trip? Where would you like to go next?

Name _____ Date _____

Endangered Species

Directions: Use the guidelines shown here and on the Perfect Paragraph Template #4 (page 92) to write an expository paper on an endangered or threatened species. Conduct your research, edit, revise, and draft a final copy.

Introduction *(3- to 5-sentence topic paragraph)*
Introduce your animal with an opinion. Why do you find it interesting? Identify at least one unique feature and one thing for which the creature is well known.

Habitat *(5- to 8-sentence paragraph)*
Tell where in the world the animal is found. Tell about its habitat, its biome, and the climate in which it lives. Tell about any adaptations it uses to survive there. Tell about the kind of nest or den it builds.

Diet *(5- to 8-sentence paragraph)*
Tell whether the animal is a carnivore, herbivore, or omnivore. Tell what it eats and how it gathers or hunts its food. What adaptations does it use to do so?

Endangerment *(5- to 8-sentence paragraph)*
Tell whether the species is threatened or endangered and why. You might also include information about what would happen if the species were to go extinct. Say what is being done to save the species, and include your opinion about what more can still be done. Conclude your paper with a sentence urging readers to help protect the species.

Multi-Paragraph Project
Imaginative
Bigfoot Encounter

Directions: Use the guidelines shown here and on the Perfect Paragraph Template #4 (page 92) to write an imaginative story in which you have an encounter with Bigfoot. Conduct research, prewrite, edit, revise, and draft a final copy.

Introduction *(3- to 5-sentence topic paragraph)*
Try to come up with a couple of sentences that *suggest* (but don't come right out and say) how something scary, unique, or mind-blowing happened to you while you were doing a certain thing. That yet-to-be-identified incident is your topic.

Set the Scene *(5- to 8-sentence paragraph)*
Lead up to the encounter by telling where you were and what you were doing. Were you hiking in the woods with your poodle? Were you having a picnic lunch in Central Park? Tell what you were hearing, seeing, and feeling.

The Encounter *(5- to 8-sentence paragraph)*
How did you encounter Bigfoot? How did you (and he) react? What thoughts went through your head? Were you afraid? Why didn't you get any pictures?

Conclusion *(5- to 8-sentence paragraph)*
How did you get out of this jam? What were you feeling when it was all over? What warning might you give others?

Letter to the Editor

Directions: Use the guidelines shown here and on the Perfect Paragraph Template #4 (page 92) to write a letter to your local paper about an issue that's important to you. Prewrite, edit, revise, and draft a final copy.

Introduction *(3- to 5-sentence topic paragraph)*
Introduce the issue and suggest that you have a solution.

The Issue *(5- to 8-sentence paragraph)*
Give details about the issue. If the issue has been around for a while, give some history. Say why the issue is important to you.

Your Solution *(5- to 8-sentence paragraph)*
Propose your solution. Why is your idea worth doing? How is it different from things that have been tried in the past?

Summarize *(5- to 8-sentence paragraph)*
Briefly restate what the issue is, what your solution is, and why others should agree with you. Conclude by urging others to take action.

Name _____   Date _____

Multi-Paragraph Project
Book Review

Storyworks Submission

Directions: Use the guidelines shown here and on the Perfect Paragraph Template #4 (page 92) to write a book review that you can submit to *Storyworks*. Read examples from *Storyworks* and then prewrite, edit, revise, and draft a final copy. When finished, mail to Book Reviews, c/o *Storyworks*, P.O. Box 712, New York, NY 10013-0712.

Introduction *(3- to 5-sentence topic paragraph)*
Introduce the book and the author, and give an overall opinion about what you've read.

The Story *(5- to 8-sentence paragraph)*
Give a summary of what happens in the book without revealing any dramatic details. Who's the main character and what's his problem?

High Points *(5- to 8-sentence paragraph)*
What is it about the book that makes you like it so much? Is it suspenseful? Does it bring you to tears or make you laugh hysterically? Is the writing especially unique?

Conclusion *(3- to 8-sentence paragraph)*
State once again how great the book is and encourage others to pick it up. You can also refer to other books by the same author.

Name _____   Date _____

Perfect Paragraph

Template #1

Basic Paragraph

Directions: Use the template to create your rough draft. Paste or write one sentence in each box.

Topic Sentence (yellow): Tells the main idea.
Supporting Sentence #1 (blue): Gives a reason, example, or event to explain the topic.
Detail Sentence #1 (green): Gives a detail about the first supporting sentence.
Supporting Sentence #2 (blue): Gives another reason, example, or event to explain the topic.
Detail Sentence #2 (green): Gives a detail about the second supporting sentence.
Conclusion Sentence (red): Repeats the main idea in different words.

Name _____

Date _____

Intermediate Paragraph

Perfect Paragraph
Template #2

Directions: Use the template to create your rough draft. Paste or write one sentence in each box.

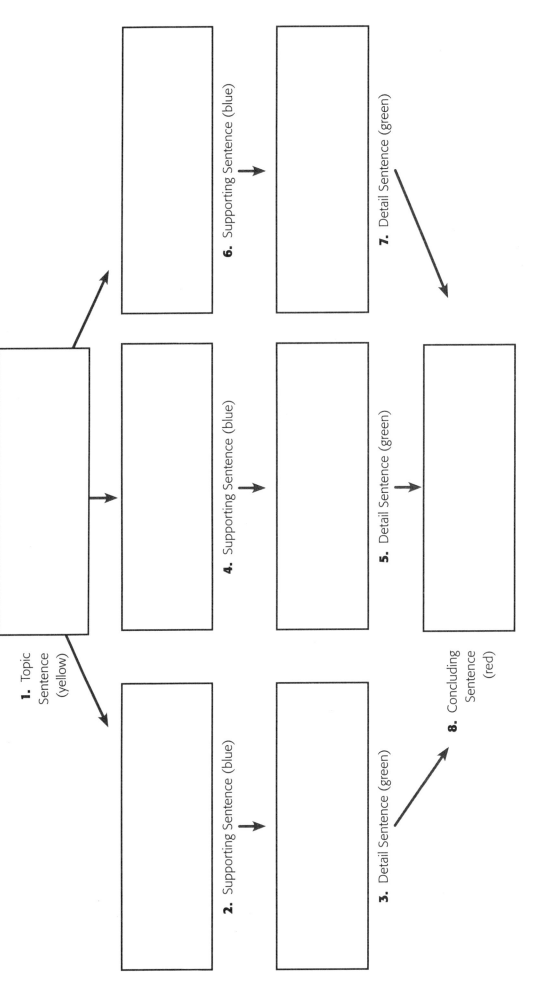

1. Topic Sentence (yellow)

2. Supporting Sentence (blue)

3. Detail Sentence (green)

4. Supporting Sentence (blue)

5. Detail Sentence (green)

6. Supporting Sentence (blue)

7. Detail Sentence (green)

8. Concluding Sentence (red)

Advanced Paragraph

Directions: Use the template to create your rough draft. Write one sentence in each box.

1. Topic Sentence (yellow)

2. Supporting Sentence (blue)

3. Detail Sentence (green)

4. Detail Sentence (green)

5. Optional: Extra Detail Sentence (green)

6. Supporting Sentence (blue)

7. Detail Sentence (green)

8. Detail Sentence (green)

9. Optional: Extra Detail Sentence (green)

10. Concluding Sentence (red)

Name _____

Date _____

Multi-Paragraph
Perfect Paragraph
Template #4

Make an enlarged copy of this sheet on 11" × 17" paper (150%).

Directions: Use the template to create your rough draft. Write one sentence in each box.

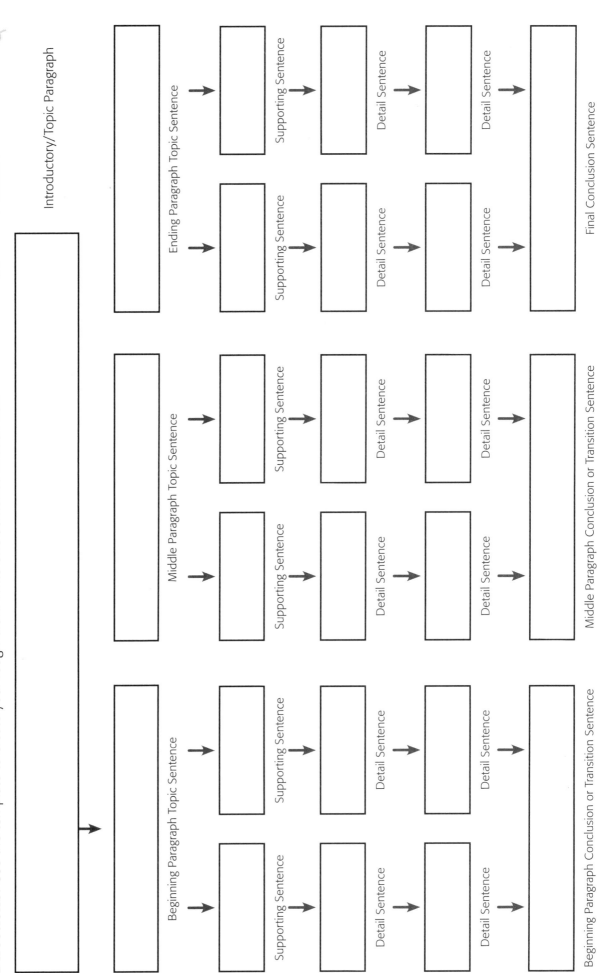

Introductory/Topic Paragraph

Beginning Paragraph Topic Sentence

Supporting Sentence

Supporting Sentence

Detail Sentence

Detail Sentence

Detail Sentence

Detail Sentence

Beginning Paragraph Conclusion or Transition Sentence

Middle Paragraph Topic Sentence

Supporting Sentence

Supporting Sentence

Detail Sentence

Detail Sentence

Detail Sentence

Detail Sentence

Middle Paragraph Conclusion or Transition Sentence

Ending Paragraph Topic Sentence

Supporting Sentence

Supporting Sentence

Detail Sentence

Detail Sentence

Detail Sentence

Detail Sentence

Final Conclusion Sentence

Super Sentences and Perfect Paragraphs © 2009 by Mack Lewis. Scholastic Teaching Resources (page 92)

Answer Key

Basic Paragraph Paste-Ups

My Crazy Cat (page 53)

My favorite pet is my cat, Buckley. One reason I like him is because he's athletic. Yesterday he climbed the screen door all the way to the ceiling. Another reason I like him is that he has crazy eyes. When he's ready to pounce, they're as big as dimes. Cats like Buckley make life more enjoyable.

A Vacation Memory (page 54)

This summer, Shelby and Cali came to my house and helped me bake a blackberry pie. We picked the berries behind the house. Shelby ate more than she put in the bucket. We used the leftover dough to make a strawberry tart. It turns out strawberries aren't so great for baking. It was wonderful having pie, but it was even better making it with my friends.

Killer Snake (page 55)

The black mamba is a fascinating species of snake. It is one of the deadliest snakes in the world. Its venom is five times as poisonous as that of the king cobra. In his book, *Going Solo*, Roald Dahl writes about the mamba. He tells how a mamba attacks his African gardener. I hope I never meet a mamba.

Horatio the Hornet (page 56)

Horatio the Hornet was getting overheated, so he tried to skim the surface of a swimming pool to get a drink. At first, the tiny droplets of water felt refreshing, but then his left wing caught a wave, and he was pulled in. Now all the water felt cold and heavy, and Horatio knew he was doomed. Suddenly, a giant blue net lifted him from the water and set him on solid ground. He heard a voice say, "These days we need all the pollinators we can get—even hornets." From then on, Horatio was one of the best pollinators around—but he was a lot more careful about where he went to cool off.

No More Broccoli (page 57)

There are some good reasons broccoli should be banned from the school cafeteria. First, broccoli may look like cute little trees, but it tastes like tree bark. The last time I tried some, I started chirping like a squirrel. Secondly, it's good for you. What kid wants to eat anything that's nutritious? That's why I think we should replace broccoli with something kids actually want, like powdered donuts.

Diary of a Spider (page 58)

Diary of a Spider by Doreen Cronin is one of those hysterically funny picture books kids of any age can enjoy. It tells what life is like for a spider, with a twist. For example, spiders and flies aren't supposed to get along, but in this book, they're best friends. My favorite part is when the spiders had a vacuum drill at school. They were taught to Stop, Drop, and Run! This book will make you laugh out loud every time you read it.

Basic Paragraph Rewrites

Thankful (page 59)

I'm thankful for many things. First of all, I'm thankful for my miniature poodle, Petunia. She plays with me after school and protects me all night. I'm also thankful for my BMX bike. Without it, I wouldn't be able to ride to the store to buy Ding Dongs. When you count your blessings like this, it's easy to feel happy.

The Worst Sick Day Ever (page 60)

My worst sick day ever was when I was in second grade. I was at school when little itchy bumps started popping up all over my body. My friend Katy started telling everyone I had zits. My mom took me out of school and drove me to Doctor Bob's office. He said I had chicken pox, so I had to rub this slimy stuff all over my body. I must have scratched for ten days straight, which is pretty awful, if you ask me.

How to Make a Sandwich (page 61)

Here's how to make a great peanut butter and jelly sandwich. The first thing you do is take out some bread and slap on some PB and J. You can use marmalade instead of jelly, but I wouldn't recommend it. Next, you stuff it in your mouth. It's pretty messy, so be prepared to do some washing up. There are probably more steps than that, but come on—who can't make a sandwich?

A Quick Trip to Mars *(page 62)*

Believe it or not, my best friend, Justin, built a spaceship out of a garbage can, a lawn-mower engine, and a box of dynamite he found in his dad's shop. We blasted into space and landed on Mars. The landing was a bit rough, but the garbage-can lid protected us. After looking around for a while, we found a Martian building a spaceship of his own. It was a lot fancier than ours. He flew us back to Earth just in time for science class.

More Time Outside *(page 63)*

I believe kids need to spend more time outside. First of all, experts say kids need more fresh air and exercise. How are we going to get it if we never see the sun? Secondly, kids get a little crazy doing schoolwork all the time. I have a friend who got so sick of grammar lessons, he started chewing a hole in his desk! Like all kids, he needs to get outdoors more often.

Runny Babbit *(page 64)*

Runny Babbit is another silly book of poetry by Shel Silverstein. It's about a group of animals that say things in a different sort of way. They swap the first letter of key words, yet once you learn the lingo, the poems make sense. One of my favorite poems in the book is "Runny's Mancy Feal." The waiter offers him crazy things like fickled pish and suna talad, but all Runny asks for is one caw rarrot. So if you'd like to bead a great rook, try *Runny Babbit*!

Intermediate Paragraph Paste-Ups

My Survival Crate *(page 65)*

If I were sailing across the Atlantic with Columbus, I would pack my crate very carefully. First of all, I would bring a secret stash of beef jerky. I have a feeling the sailors get a bit hungry on those trips. Next, I'd bring a harmonica. I've always wanted to learn it, and with a month at sea, I'd have plenty of time. Finally, I'd be sure to bring some long underwear. Two pairs would be even better. If I had all that stuff, I might just make it.

River Kayaks *(page 66)*

Last summer, I had a great time kayaking down the river. We rented kayaks and put in at a place called Graves Creek. The kayaks looked a little like torpedoes. At first, the river was slow and calm, which was great for spotting wildlife. I saw a bald eagle make off with a fish, and three deer standing on a sandbar. Pretty soon, the river started running wild. I thought the rapids would swallow me alive. That was an outdoor adventure I'll never forget.

Bully for Teddy Roosevelt *(page 67)*

Theodore Roosevelt is one of the most fascinating people in American history. He's famous for leading the charge up San Juan Hill during the Spanish-American War, but did you know he also saved football? He helped make the sport safer so that it would not be banned. In addition to sports, he also loved the outdoors and worked hard to protect nature. While president, he created the National Forest system and preserved more than 200 million acres of land, including much of the Grand Canyon. Finally, the Teddy Bear is named after Roosevelt. He refused to shoot a captured bear during a hunting trip, and all of America cheered him for it. There is a lot more to know about Theodore Roosevelt, but it's already easy to see why his face is carved on Mount Rushmore.

Inside My Video Game! *(page 68)*

On Saturday, I was playing my PS2 when somehow I got sucked into Need for Speed, the video game. I was ripping through San Francisco in a supercharged Mustang. It was blue with green flames on the side, and it had a massive Nitrous Oxide System in back. The car I was racing skidded out in front of me, so I hung a quick left. The turn sent me heading toward a drawbridge that was opening. I punched the NOS switch and blasted my way across the gap. Green flames came bursting out of my tailpipe as I flew through the air. It was quite a ride, and when I woke up on the sofa, I was all sweaty.

Vote for Me! *(page 69)*

I think I should be our next class president. First of all, I'm a good listener. When my friends come to me with their complaints, I always pay attention. Another good reason to elect me is that I'm not afraid to talk to the principal. When our class wants to make big changes, I'll be willing to meet with him myself. Lastly, I'll bring donuts to class once a month. Glazed, chocolate-covered, powdered, those ones with all the sprinkles on them—you'll have your choice! So vote for me, the good-listening, principal-talking, donut-bringing candidate!

Super Sentences and Perfect Paragraphs © 2009 by Mack Lewis. Scholastic Teaching Resources

Holes *(page 70)*

If you haven't seen *Holes*, the movie, you've been cheated! It stars Shia LaBeouf as Stanley Yelnats. He's not quite what I imagined Stanley would look like, but he does a great job with the part. One reason I liked the movie is that it follows the book's story line almost exactly. I think that's because Louis Sachar, the author, is also the screenwriter. Another reason is that the bad guys are all so nasty. The Warden, Mr. Sir, and Mr. Pendanski are all perfectly cast. It's not as good as the book, but I give this flick two thumbs up!

Intermediate Paragraph Rewrites

The Coolest Room *(page 71)*

My room is special to me because it's full of fantastic sights and sounds. For one thing, I have lots of wrestling posters tacked to my ceiling. When I'm lying in bed, I imagine myself body slamming Stone Cold Steve Austin. I also have a cage full of gerbils. At night, it's comforting to hear them scratching in the sawdust and shredded paper. Finally, my bunk bed is like a jungle gym. Sometimes I pretend I'm a monkey swinging from bunk to bunk. I guess I'm pretty lucky to have such a cool room.

A Lame Halloween *(page 72)*

This year, I had the lamest Halloween ever. First of all, my mom made me go to school wearing the same Pokemon costume I wore last year. The kids all laughed at me when they saw the silly yellow fur and the big, round eyes. Next, the teacher cancelled the class party. He made us watch a movie about brushing our teeth instead. Finally, when I went trick-or-treating at the mall, all they gave out were three-year-old Tootsie Rolls. I cracked a tooth when I tried to chew one. Yep, it was definitely a holiday worth forgetting.

An Important Event in History *(page 73)*

A great moment in history was when Harriett Beecher Stowe wrote *Uncle Tom's Cabin*. It was important because it showed the country what slavery was really like. It was a huge best-seller, and after reading it, many people started calling for the abolition of slavery. It may even have convinced President Abraham Lincoln to fight. When Lincoln met Stowe, he said, "So you're the little lady that started this great big war." Stowe's book also shows how important it is to be able to write well. Through her words, she helped end slavery. Imagine how different our country might have been had she never written those words!

The Day I Met Elvis *(page 74)*

I was fishing for walleye on a lake outside of town when Elvis Presley came rowing up in a canoe. He introduced himself, and then he asked me what kind of bait I was using. It was eerie hearing him say his name in that famous Southern drawl. I told him I was using a lure, and I showed him my collection. He seemed particularly taken with my willowspoon jig, so I let him have it. I asked him where he'd been all these years. "I just been layin' low" is all he said, and then he paddled away. To this day, I wonder if he ever caught anything with my jig.

An Energizing Breakfast *(page 75)*

There are lots of reasons to eat breakfast. First of all, a good breakfast gives you lots of energy. One time, I skipped breakfast and then fell asleep during a spelling test! A good breakfast also builds strong bones. I always have milk in the morning, which gives me calcium. Finally, a good breakfast keeps me from getting hungry during class. I never need a snack when I have bacon with breakfast. I think breakfast is the most important meal of the day.

Boy *(page 76)*

When you read *Boy*, which is about Roald Dahl's childhood in boarding school, you see where he got a lot of the ideas for his books. I like this book because you're never sure what's going to happen next. For instance, when Roald gets most of his nose cut off, I almost fell out of my chair! In another story, the Matron pours soap in the mouth of a snoring boy. The Matron reminds me of the Trunchbull in *Matilda*. Finally, there's also the tale about how Roald and his friends put a dead mouse in the Gobstopper jar. The store's owner almost has a heart attack, but Roald's punishment is even worse. This is a hilarious book that makes you glad you don't go to boarding school!

Advanced Paragraph Rewrites

Cell Phone Fever *(page 77)*

I just got the best cell phone ever! It does all the usual stuff, but it also downloads videos from the Internet at the touch of a button. Yesterday, I watched YouTube until my battery died! The best video was about a girl whose cell phone overheated and caught her purse on fire. My cell phone also has GPS, which means my friends can track me down anywhere on earth. If I ever get lost in Siberia, somebody will be able to find me. How I'd end up in Siberia is anybody's guess. Lastly, it has text messaging in 18 languages. Nothing drives my friends crazier than when I text them in Chinese. Half the time I don't know what I'm saying to them, but my cell phone seems to. It would be even better if I could figure out how to place a call, but with all these other great features to keep me busy, who has time to talk on the phone anyway?

My First Date (page 78)

On Saturday, I went on a date with my new boyfriend, Alvin. First, his mom drove us to the movie theater so we could see *Gilligan's Island: The Next Generation*. It's about how all Gilligan's grandkids get shipwrecked. I thought the story was really stupid, but Alvin was practically rolling around in the aisle laughing hysterically! Next, Alvin took me to lunch at the McDonald's across the street. After he had scarfed down his second Big Mac, I noticed he had something disgusting stuck between his teeth. It made me sick, and now that's all I can think about when I look at Alvin. I guess that's what you get when you mess around with boys.

Homemade Soup From a Can (page 79)

Making homemade soup is easy if you know the steps. First, you open the can. I look for cans with pop-tops so that I don't have to use a can opener. Next, you pour the soup into a bowl. You should make sure the bowl is safe for the microwave. After that, you put it in the microwave and press a few buttons. Some microwave ovens have one button that says "soup." Finally, you take it out and chow down. I just love Chicken With Stars. Okay, maybe it isn't really homemade, but it tastes great and it's easy to fix!

Why I Invented the Phlurg (page 80)

Hasbro has just paid me over a million dollars for my newest invention, the Phlurg. The Phlurg is a container you can put your gum in when you're not chewing it. It injects freshness into the gum so that when you go to munch on it again, it still tastes great. One big benefit is that it will keep you out of trouble. When the playground monitor starts looking at you funny, you can turn away and slip your gum into the Phlurg. That way you can safely hide it in your pocket before anyone is the wiser. The Phlurg also helps keep the planet green. Instead of sticking your wad under your desk or tossing it on the sidewalk, you can store it in your Phlurg. Check out the Phlurg at select retailers everywhere!

Reasons for a Water Bottle (page 81)

There are lots of reasons to bring your own water bottle to school. For one thing, it means you don't have to drink the nasty stuff coming out of the school's rusty pipes. One time, I drank too much of it, and it made me sick. The nurse made me drink half a bottle of Pepto Bismol! Also, having your own water bottle means you don't have to get up to get a drink. Why go through all that trouble just because you're thirsty? Finally, if somebody's bugging you, you can bop him on the head or squirt him in the eye. Be careful, though, because that could land you in the principal's office. I think having a water bottle is a good idea.

Harris and Me (page 82)

Harris and Me by Gary Paulsen is totally crazy! I like this book because you never know what Harris is going to do next. When he hooked a washing-machine motor to a bicycle, I laughed my head off. His overalls got torn off him in the crash! In another chapter, Harris pretends he's Tarzan and jumps out of the hayloft. He lands on a pig and gets attacked by his family's evil rooster, Ernie. The book is also full of great characters, such as Harris's sister, Glennis. Whenever Harris cusses—which he does a lot—she smacks him upside the head. This book is a scream and makes you wish you were related to a "gooner" like Harris! You should read it!